MCR

22.45

MCR

DEC - 1 2005

DATE DUE

JUL 2 6 2006	
MAY 2 4 2008	

DEMCO, INC. 38-2931

TRADING CARDS

From Start to Finish

Ryan A. Smith

Photographs by Gary Tolle

BLACKBIRCH PRESS

An imprint of Thomson Gale, a part of The Thomson Corporation

THOMSON

GALE

Detroit • New York • San Francisco • San Diego • New Haven, Conn. • Waterville, Maine • London • Munich

For more information, contact
Blackbirch Press
27500 Drake Rd.
Farmington Hills, MI 48331-3535
Or you can visit our Internet site at www.gale.com

Photo Credits: Cover, all photos © Gary Tolle, except page 3 © Bettmann/CORBIS; page 4 (inset) © Getty Images; pages 4 (background), 22 (background), 23, 25, 26 (inset), 28 (background), 29 (background) © Jim Pidgeon; pages 5 (inset), 6, 8, 9 (inset), 10, 13 Courtesy of The Upper Deck Company, LLC

LIBRARY OF CONGRESS CATALOGING-IN-PUBLICATION DATA

Smith, Ryan A., 1974–
 Trading cards / by Ryan A. Smith.
   p. cm. — (Made in the USA)
 ISBN 1-4103-0374-8 (hardcover : alk. paper)
 1. Sports cards—Juvenile literature. I. Title. II. Series: Made in the U.S.A.

GV568.5.S52 2005
796'.075—dc22   2004023177

Printed in United States
10 9 8 7 6 5 4 3 2 1

Contents

Dedication
For my grandparents: The Mirandas, Lichtmans, and Smiths.

Special Thanks
Special thanks to Gary Tolle, Steve Berns, Kerri Stockholm, Louise Curcio, Jim Pidgeon, Jake Gonzales, Mike Eggleston, and the hundreds of people working at Upper Deck.

Upper Deck is the world's premier trading card company.

Upper Deck

Upper Deck is a leading sports trading card manufacturer. Upper Deck cards are sold in countries throughout Europe, Asia, and North America.

The Upper Deck facility in Carlsbad is huge. The main building alone is over 250,000 square feet (23,226 square meters), about the size of 100 houses! Upper Deck never closes, and people sometimes work in shifts all day and through the night. Inside Upper Deck, sports trading cards are conceived, designed, digitally created, printed, packaged, and shipped.

Left: Design elements have replaced the background on this football card.
Right: This basketball card shows the player in a game environment.

Designing Trading Cards

Designers have ideas in mind about what the cards should look like. First the design is drawn on paper. Then the sketch is re-created using computer graphics programs. Design elements include different textures, colors, backgrounds, and print types.

The designer also decides whether to show the player in an actual game surrounding or to replace the background with design elements instead.

The finished design is printed and becomes a colorful mechanical. A mechanical is an elaborate set of plans. It displays the series design like a blueprint. It also gives written instructions to different departments about the cards, colors, logos, layout, and content.

Right: *A designer creates a mechanical using a computer.*
Below: *A mechanical is a set of plans and instructions for each series.*

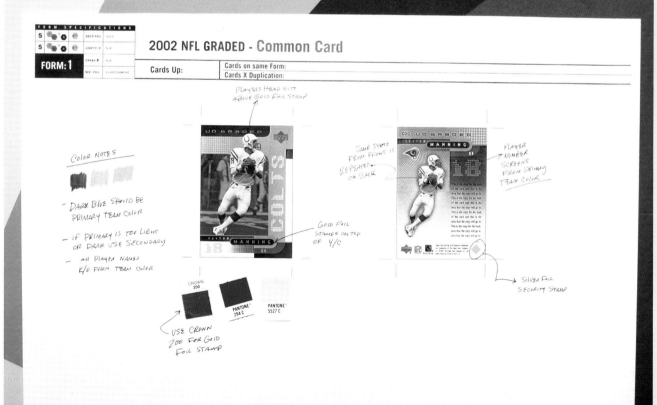

Pictures

Over a million pictures are sent to Upper Deck every year for sports trading cards. Photographers from all over the United States schedule photo shoots with professional athletes to capture hundreds of pictures per hour. Sometimes photographers will take action shots of athletes during games. Other times an entire sports team will have thousands of portraits taken in a single day!

Photographers take action pictures of professional basketball player LeBron James.

A photo editor views several pictures of a player (inset) using a searchable database.

The photo department at Upper Deck primarily uses digital pictures. Photographers send images to Upper Deck on compact discs (CDs) or over the Internet as digital computer picture files.

When a player's picture is selected, all of the athlete's pictures are uploaded, or placed, from the CDs onto a searchable database. Photo editors can find pictures on a computer screen by entering keywords, specifications, or image codes. Photo editors look at hundreds, even thousands, of pictures for each unique card.

HT: 6'1"   WT: 220   BORN: 1.15.79   COLLEGE: PURDUE

YR	TEAM	ATT	COM	PCT	YDS	LG	TD	INT	RYDS	TDS
01	CHARGERS	27	15	55.6	221	40	1	0	18	0
02	CHARGERS	526	320	60.8	3284	52	17	16	130	1
03	CHARGERS	356	205	57.6	2108	68	11	15	84	0
3-Year Totals		909	540	59.4	5613	68	29	31	232	1

Despite not having speedy receivers to utilize, Brees was still able to post solid numbers in 2003. An accurate passer, Brees eclipsed 3,000 yards in 2002.

Type

Writers at Upper Deck begin creating minibiographies of the athletes a week after the trading card picture is chosen. Writers gather information and statistics for every player using books, magazines, and the Internet.

Writers collect statistics and write a biography for each player's trading card.

Trading Cards

For more than a century, kids and adults alike have collected trading cards. Today, sports trading cards are a global industry, and are created for professional sports such as baseball, football, basketball, hockey, golf, and soccer.

But how are sports trading cards made?

Kids and adults have collected trading cards for over 100 years.

History of Baseball Cards

Baseball cards are the most popular trading cards to date. Historians say baseball cards were first produced in 1869. Back then, cards were placed inside tobacco products to boost sales, like small toys are added into cereal boxes today. Later, in the 1920s and 1930s, a few candy and gum companies began inserting baseball cards into their packages. But the modern era of baseball cards started in 1948, when the Bowman Gum Company packaged and sold one card and one stick of gum for one penny.

Today, some trading cards are worth many thousands of dollars or more. The most valuable card in the world is a mint condition, or flawless, Honus Wagner from the early 1900s. Only one mint condition Wagner card exists, and it recently sold for over 1 million dollars!

WAGNER, PITTSBURG

A copy editor proofreads the content and statistics of sports trading cards.

Once the writing is complete, the content and statistics for the trading card are proofread by copy editors. The editors refer to the mechanical to make sure all the words and statistics will fit inside the card designs.

A graphic artist creates a baseball card using computer graphics programs.

The Production Department

The production department receives the work of the designers, photo editors, and writers, and creates each unique card as shown on the mechanical.

A graphic artist makes a sports trading card one side at a time using computer graphics programs. Bases, or layers, are added to a player's picture to create each card.

The background design is on the first layer

The player picture is on the second layer

The foil stamp is on the third layer

A base contains one visual element of the trading card, like the logo, color band, shadow, or outline. Bases are piled onto each other, one by one, until the trading card viewed onscreen looks finished.

Then the graphic artist makes the back of the card in the same way, adding graphic elements, the player's career statistics, and a short biography. The front and back of a single sports trading card can sometimes require as many as 25 bases!

The graphic artist piles layers of elements, or bases, onto each other to give each card a unique look.

Upper Deck History

In 1989, Upper Deck officially entered the sports trading card market with a series of glossy baseball cards constructed with advanced printing techniques. The first cards instantly became favorites among serious collectors and enabled the small company to grow rapidly.

In the time since, Upper Deck has become the largest sports trading card company in the world. Upper Deck currently produces sports trading cards for professional baseball, football, basketball, hockey, soccer, and golf.

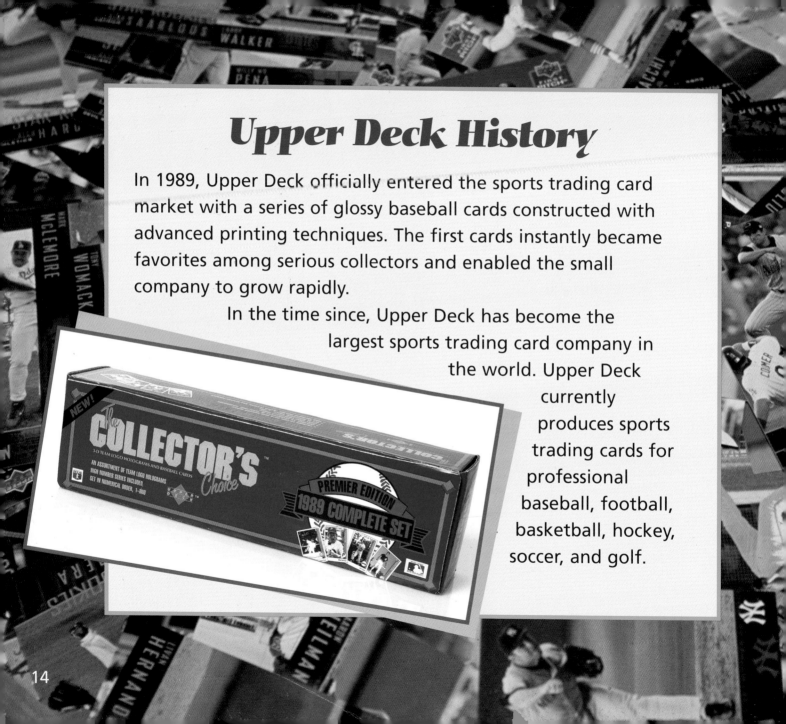

Sometimes Upper Deck designs and produces 40,000 unique sports trading cards in a single year.

Upper Right: *The 1989 Ken Griffey Jr. baseball card is the most recognizable trading card from Upper Deck.*
Lower Right: *Today Upper Deck makes trading cards for six major sports.*

Ken Griffey Jr.

Intermediate proofs go to several departments at Upper Deck for accuracy checks.

Proofing

Once a graphic artist has completed building a unique card on a computer, an intermediate proof, or layered blueprint, of the card is made using expensive color printers. An intermediate proof is almost like the series mechanical, but the proof shows the many bases on the front and back of each trading card. All of the card's contents are also shown, including the player picture, colors, logos, color bands, and player info. The intermediate proof is routed to several departments within Upper Deck, and to the professional sports league, so the card can be checked for quality and accuracy.

A graphic artist color corrects a picture.

Color Correction

While the intermediate proof is being routed, each card's picture must go through a process called color correction. During the process, a graphic artist slightly adjusts the colors of a digital picture to better reflect true-to-life tones, if necessary. Color correcting helps ensure the highest quality picture files are used for sports trading cards every time.

Plating

The characteristics of every sports trading card must be captured onto a plate so that the card can be printed onto cardboard paper. Each plate is a large, thin sheet of specialized aluminum that has been etched inside advanced printerlike machines. Like a regular computer printer, these machines receive digital codes and instructions that describe the look of the card from a computer network. Where a regular printer would use ink,

A sheet of aluminum is loaded into an etching machine to become a printing plate.

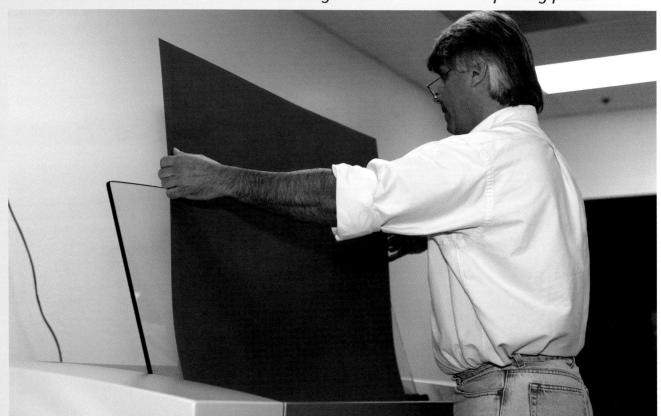

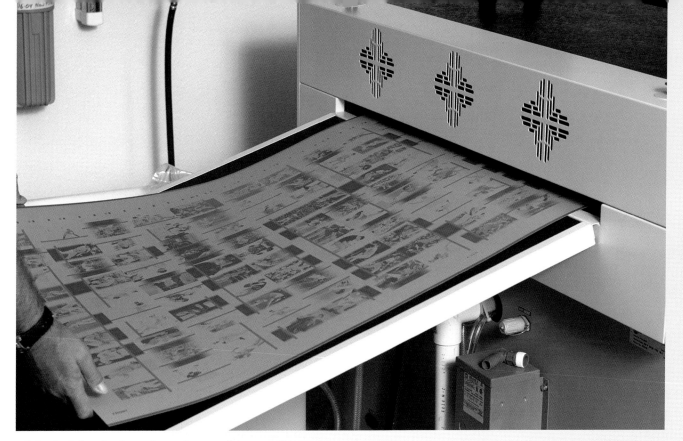

This finished plate has the etchings of over 100 sports trading cards.

though, the machines use a laser and emulsion process to etch the features of each card into aluminum plates. Some plates simultaneously hold the etchings of up to 110 trading cards.

Each completed plate shows one side of the trading cards backward, and will be used like a rubber stamp inside the massive printing presses at the next stage. The back of the cards must also be plated before the sports trading cards can be printed.

Print

Giant printing presses are used to create the cardboard sports trading cards sold in stores. A pressman controls the printing presses. The plates are delivered from production to the pressman and loaded into the press. A list of ink color codes is also given to the pressman, telling him or her the exact colors to use during the printing process.

Once the printing press is turned on, the plates and inks are pressed onto large sheets of thick paper, creating glossy, multicolored sheets of trading

A printing press uses paper, plates, and ink to create sheets of cards.

cards. The plates and ink codes are changed inside the press after the print run is completed. The newly printed sheets of cards are turned over and sent through the press again to have the back side printed.

A press check usually occurs after the first sheets of cards are completely printed. Upper Deck's design and production managers carefully inspect the newly printed cards to make sure each one looks perfect. If the sheets are approved, the rest of the sports trading card series will be printed.

A pressman inspects a newly printed sheet of cards.

Print Materials

Millions of dollars worth of paper and ink are required for Upper Deck to make sports trading cards for a single year. More than 7 million sheets of cardboard paper are used during an average year. Upper Deck also uses six different colors of ink to make sports trading cards. Nearly

100,000 gallons (378,541l) of ink are delivered to the Carlsbad facility annually. That is enough ink to fill the gas tanks of more than 5,000 midsized trucks!

Opposite: *Stored paper and cans of ink soon become trading cards.*
Upper Right: *Heavy stacks of paper are delivered to the printers.*
Lower: *Tons of paper are used at Upper Deck each year.*

The Cutter

The approved sheets of sports trading cards are sent to the cutter machine. Inside the cutter, razor-sharp blades automatically cut through tall stacks of card sheets. Each card is cut to 2.5 inches wide by 3.5 inches tall (6.35cm by 8.89cm).

A technician feeds printed sheets of trading cards into the cutter machine.

Individual cards are placed into cardboard boxes called sleeves.

The thousands of individual trading cards are then neatly gathered and placed into long, slim cardboard boxes called sleeves. When the sleeves are completely filled, they are transported to the hoppers.

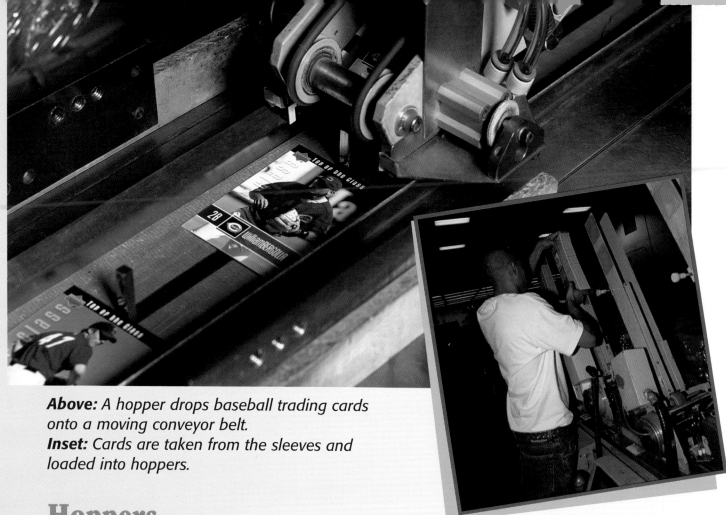

Above: *A hopper drops baseball trading cards onto a moving conveyor belt.*
Inset: *Cards are taken from the sleeves and loaded into hoppers.*

Hoppers

The cards are taken out of the sleeves and loaded into hoppers. Rows of hoppers are connected by a long conveyor belt. As the conveyor belt moves from beginning to end, the hoppers randomly drop the trading cards into the moving line of cards. Some specialty trading cards are also dropped in line by specially programmed hoppers as an added bonus for collectors.

The Wrap Machine

As the lines of sports trading cards move toward the end of the conveyor belts, the cards are fed into the wrap machine. The wrap machine is programmed to collect the cards into stacks and seal them in slim packages. Each series has its own package design, and contains between 3 and 24 sports trading cards, depending on the series. The new packages of sports trading cards are lowered onto the conveyor belt and dropped onto a table at its end.

Cards are sealed in a slim package (inset) inside the wrap machine (below).

High-Quality Cards

In 1989, the Upper Deck Company introduced a new era of high-quality sports trading cards with its first baseball series. Using advanced design and printing techniques, the early trading cards featured a glossy look highlighted by an Upper Deck hologram. The hologram was originally designed as a method to prevent counterfeits from being produced, and as a recognizable trademark of the company.

Upper Deck has continued to make advances in sports trading cards over the years. Adding to the collectibility of Upper Deck cards, several specialty series cards are created. Specialty cards are the most valuable sports trading cards in each series, and are inserted into every so many packages. For example, 1 particular specialty card may

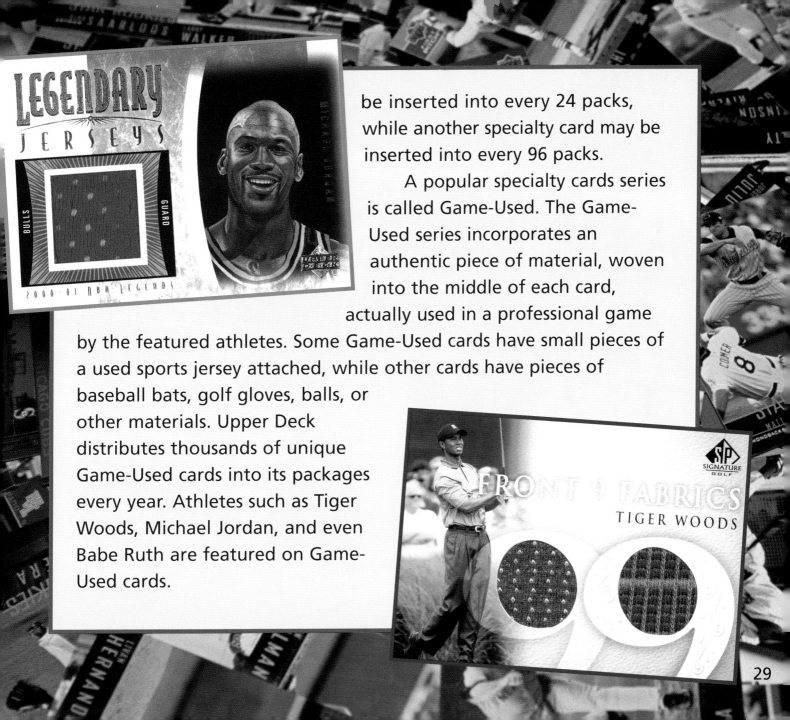

be inserted into every 24 packs, while another specialty card may be inserted into every 96 packs.

A popular specialty cards series is called Game-Used. The Game-Used series incorporates an authentic piece of material, woven into the middle of each card, actually used in a professional game by the featured athletes. Some Game-Used cards have small pieces of a used sports jersey attached, while other cards have pieces of baseball bats, golf gloves, balls, or other materials. Upper Deck distributes thousands of unique Game-Used cards into its packages every year. Athletes such as Tiger Woods, Michael Jordan, and even Babe Ruth are featured on Game-Used cards.

Box and Ship

The packages of cards at the end of the conveyor belt are collected manually and placed directly into display boxes that hold 20 or 25 packages each. The display boxes are sealed, packaged in large cardboard boxes, and delivered to sellers around the world.

After several months of manufacturing, the latest series of sports trading cards become available to the public once delivered and placed onto store shelves. There, they are purchased by collectors eagerly hoping the next package contains one of their favorite players, or even tomorrow's Honus Wagner!

Opposite: Display boxes filled with football cards are prepared for shipping.
Inset: A forklift loads boxes of trading cards into a delivery truck.

Glossary

Base A digital layer added during the production process to make sports trading cards

Collectibility Increased value

Game-Used cards Sports trading cards inserted with small pieces of professionally used sports equipment

Hopper A machine used to randomly drop sports trading cards before being packaged

Intermediate proof A layered set of plans made for each unique card

Mechanical A template or elaborate blueprint

Mint condition Perfect, in its original, unused condition, as if new

Plate A large, thin sheet of aluminum used to capture the features of each card

Upload To transfer data from a small computer

For More Information

Books

James Beckett. *Official Beckett Price Guide to Baseball Cards 2004.* New York: House of Collectibles, 2004.

Web Sites

The Upper Deck Company, LLC
(www.upperdeck.com). The official Web site of Upper Deck company.

DCS Sports Cards
(www.dcssportscards.com/baseballcards.html). A history of baseball cards.

Index